Plains
Animals

by **Sharon Gordon**

Reading Consultant: Nanci R. Vargus, Ed.D.

Marshall Cavendish
Benchmark
New York

Picture Words

 aardvark

 animals

 cheetah

 elephant

 giraffe

lion

 ostrich

 trunk

 zebras

The of the African plains are busy.

The digs with its claws.

The jumps with its strong legs.

The 🦒 eats with its long tongue.

The sprays water with its .

The drink water with their herd.

The plays with its cub.

The runs with its long legs.

What busy
they are!

Words to Know

busy (BIZ-ee)
    at work

herd   a number of animals that move
        together

plains (planes)
        flat, open land

sprays
            to move tiny drops of water
            through the air

Find Out More

Books

Dunphy, Madeleine. *Here Is the African Savanna*. Berkeley, CA: Web of Life Children's Books, 2007.

Rau, Dana Meachen. *The Lion in the Grass*. New York: Benchmark Books, 2007.

Schuette, Sarah L. *African Animals ABC: An Alphabet Safari*. Mankato, MN: Capstone Books, 2003.

DVD

SVE & Churchill Media (Firm). *Biomes for Students: Grasslands*. Science & math video discoveries. [S.l.]: SVE & Churchill Media, 2004.

Web Sites

African Savanna
www.Nationalzoo.si.edu/Animals/AfricanSavanna/afsavkids.cfm

National Geographic Kids: Animal Creature Features
www.kids.nationalgeographic.com/Animals/Creature Feature/

About the Author

Sharon Gordon is an author, advertising copywriter, and editor. She is a graduate of Montclair State University in New Jersey and has written over 100 children's books, many for Marshall Cavendish, which include works of fiction, nonfiction, and cultural history. Along with her family, she enjoys exploring the plant and animal wildlife of the Outer Banks of North Carolina.

About the Reading Consultant

Nanci R. Vargus, Ed.D., wants all children to enjoy reading. She used to teach first grade. Now she works at the University of Indianapolis. Nanci helps young people become teachers. She will explore many plains animals on her next vacation, an African safari.

Marshall Cavendish Benchmark
99 White Plains Road
Tarrytown, NY 10591-5502
www.marshallcavendish.us

All Internet addresses were correct at the time of printing.

Library of Congress Cataloging-in-Publication Data
Gordon, Sharon.
Plains animals / by Sharon Gordon.
       p. cm. — (Benchmark Rebus. Animals in the wild)
Summary: "Easy to read text with rebuses explores animals that live in the plains"—Provided by publisher.
Includes bibliographical references.
ISBN 978-0-7614-2902-9
Plains animals—Juvenile literature. I. Title.
QL115.G67 2009
591.74—dc22
       2007042213

Editor: Christine Florie
Publisher: Michelle Bisson
Art Director: Anahid Hamparian
Series Designer: Virginia Pope

Photo research by Connie Gardner

Rebus images, with the exception of aardvark, provided courtesy of *Dorling Kindersley*.

Cover photo by Polka Dot Images/SuperStock

The photographs in this book are used with permission and through the courtesy of:
Animals, Animals, p. 2 (aardvark); *Minden Pictures:* p. 5 Martin Harvey/Foto Natura; p. 11 Anup Shah/npl;
pp. 15, 21 Frans Lanting; p. 17 Suzi Eszterhas; *SuperStock:* p. 7 age footstock; *Art Life Images:* p. 9 age footstock;
Getty Images: p. 13 Heinrich Van den Berg; *Peter Arnold:* p. 19 Bios photo/Denis-Huot Michel and Christine.

Printed in Malaysia
1   3   5   6   4   2